I0381503

AN IMPORTANT SKY

Poems

KEVIN J. FELLOWS

Modern Folklore Press

Copyright

Names, characters, places, and incidents are products of the author's imagination or are used fictitiously and are not to be considered as real. Any resemblance to actual events, locales, organizations or persons, living or dead, is entirely coincidental.

An Important Sky
Poems by Kevin J. Fellows
Copyright © 2020 Kevin J. Fellows

First Edition
ISBN: 978-1-7351300-2-6

All rights reserved. Modern Folklore Press and the author provide this book to you for your personal use only. Except for brief quotations embodied in critical articles and reviews, you may not make this book publicly available in anyway. Such duplication and distribution is a violation of copyright law.

For information, address:
Modern Folklore Press
PO Box 230681
Las Vegas, NV 89105

Dedication

To my friends and family who live or have lived on granite,
under an important sky.

Contents

Winter's Bone	1
My Sport	3
Thaw	5
A River Runs	7
Red River	9
Promise	11
Coffee	13
Schemes and Plans	15
The Gifts of Age	17
All the Things	19
Underwear	20
Underwear	21
Our Broken Lands	23
Ancestors' Absence	25
No Accident	27
Elegy for Piano and Harp	29
The Wood Stove	31
Shadows of '32	33
My Grandmother's Place	34
Birds Unknown to Me	37
New Hampshire Haiku	39
Peeling Grapes	41
What the Wind Hears	43
Stand Still	45
Quiet Days	47
Laughter in the Sky	48
An Important Sky	50
Bibliography	53
Acknowledgments	55
About the Author	57
Also by Kevin J. Fellows	59

Winter's Bone

The wind of winter's last
steals my breath,
careens it forward,
a fierce and lonely blast

Shards of withered white
gleans my eye,
drags me backward,
a dark, searing light

The memory of winter's bone
pricks my chest,
casts me downward,
my failure to atone

My Sport

Winter's crust is a shell; skinned
over by rain and ice
sealing the downy snow; a sheen
of white cake icing

We make a sport of skating
Rising, dipping, swooping, careening
between trees at hair-raising speed; leaning
into the curve around the
half buried barrow; gliding
on blades cross-country

Thaw

I will eat the bones of that winter,
of October and April
It lasted a lifetime as
ice in my mouth
Cold pain behind my eyes
freezing my jaw

Will my brother
find his rest unburied
until the thaw

A River Runs

My river cuts through hills and fields,
falls fresh from the mountain's tower
rushing slowly to another day

Pools eddy in deepening cold; memories of winter
Jagged rapids slice until bleeding white; turn and twist

Swirls of leaves float among ripples
Mud seethes on the shore
Trees tower and moan; reflecting

Shadows mirror a sky, clear blue,
clouded gray, and starlit black
Stones tumble ages from their lofty mountain start

Fish hide until called to the fly
I'm planted on this bridge, drawn to the flow,
and all that flows is black

Red River

Red river ranges

rollicking robust
rolling roundly,

roughly reduced
remade,

red river renewed

Promise

The promise of a warm early sun
falls prey to a cold late moon
Returning to try again
in the pale fires
of tomorrow

Coffee

The coffee's not hot enough to burn away the sleep
clinging to my eyes as pitch to a branch,
tacking my vision

The world remains distant; not present
before my sleep-wrinkled face

I'm caught in the realm where dreams have fled
and thoughts have not yet flooded

A lonely space where cares and worry
work their dread through the long,
rapid hours of the day

Schemes and Plans

In the small of the day,
when the hours are wee
and thoughts are grand

The first to see
light stretch over land;
I find my way and make
my plan

Until the long late hours
reveal my schemes lacking;
their logic too small to withstand
the scrutiny of my hands

The Gifts of Age

Pain rises; flares in my sinew
Coils of fire constrict my knee,
shoulder, or foot

Floating stains roll across my eyes;
spots spoil my skin
Youth evaporated from my exterior

These gifts; my rewards granted
for living to see
this length of years

All the Things

All the things I don't have can fill the world
No car, no gym membership,
no meals delivered in kits or bags
None of those things I want

Of all the things I do not have,
the only thing I wish,
is the means to live
without the things I do not have

Underwear

Racing homeward, the road a blurred vista
of rocks, mountains, and sheep.

Miles sweep dust under the wheels.
Gold sunlight breaks clouds and
fires the jagged red edges of a hard landscape.

Snatches of color wink by:
the pale green abandoned trailer,
the rusted red gas pumps,
and a broken orange sign.

Underwear

A glimpse of red; a warning.
Not a red flag—but a woman's thong
wrapped atop a mileage post.

A prank, or something sinister?

Am I jaded for thinking such;
for imagining awful things?

Our Broken Lands

Fallow;
ice scarred and sun scorched
untilled and untillable,
thrush, worn, and wasted

Bones of the land,
grow inward from the shore

White coral sand blossoms
and burns at the edges;
dry, blasted

our broken lands

Ancestors' Absence

There's a memory of a memory lost
We killed ourselves and buried our ancestors
We renounced living free for beggared farms
where we sold long memories
in a currency we lacked

Better to die in the colony's life;
to pray to their god who was our god;
the one they didn't recognize

We remember who we were; not who we are
No bridge breaches that gap
Our children and their children see
only empty forgotten spaces marking
the absence of our fathers and their blood

No Accident

When the darkness folds his dreams
into the loss that lasts a lifetime;
those who did the deed forget.
Just a job; a match and well-placed
kerosene.

Accident. The child re-lives
the dark burning midnight screams
burning him, scorching me.
The loss that lasts a lifetime
draws scars through intent;
no accident.

Elegy for Piano and Harp

I loathe slow piano solos
and a lone harp's numb trill
So cold and lonely;
plink and pluck,
followed by hollow echoes

Warm me instead with the hum
of strings
Wrap me in soft washes;
heal me with warm waves pulsing
from my father's wood-stove

The Wood Stove

Forests
stacked
and piled,
sawn and

split

Repose under the seething sun
drying and cracking,
sometimes snapping in parching
throes beyond death

Each tree carefully gathered
for its winter funeral in our house

one
chunk
at
a
time

Shadows of '32

Shadows of the hurricane;
the rage of '32 and its swift black flood
imprinted in her memory.

Like the high-water mark etched
above our heads
on the old A&P and the five & dime.

We walk over a bridge of granite
bearing her flower boxes
lovingly tended.

A granite bridge replaced the broken, wooden sticks
of the old—washed under the covered rail bridge,
eddied downriver—clogged.

Night terrors stamped on my young gram.
Swirling water, sweeping death and damage
in darkness again and again.
But we loved the ocean.

My Grandmother's Place

On the bus I peeled frosted windows into snow
to see the train resting for spring
and the work of uprooting its own tracks

The Boston mafia deposited bodies
in burned cars and steel barrels in the woods;
broke the arm of a family friend

The Memorial Day Parade where annually I sweat
in suit and tie
propaganda for a glory
that never was
is now a sham of even this

My grandmother left me blooming fields
with cows and orchards of ripe apples
flowing spring sap
and the sharp snap
of fresh green beans

My Grandmother's Place

There are glimpses now and then on a snowy night;
flakes blossoming in the glow of soft, quiet lights
Soundless echoes only
of the place grandmother left for me

Birds Unknown to Me

I hear the wind
sifting through trees
and birds unfamiliar call

Creatures unreal,
darting, soaring
grubbing with grace

Their names spelled out
in movement and sound;
hopping
soaring, chirping, cawing

Or painted head and face,
striped tails and flaming beak
I see them every day
These birds unknown to me

New Hampshire Haiku

1

Forlorn the loon sounds
Moose thumps and tramps silently
Trout floats in crystal

2

Blue mountain gray skies
Soft earth under leaves; ice, snow
Pine pinches my nose

3

Red, orange, burn the green
Harsh winds push; turn the seasons
Leaf breaks; falls alone

Peeling Grapes

The old man peels the skin, barely anything; thin
He does it carefully with slow and steady hands
A knife worn; whet and honed a hundred times
He peels the skin from grapes
with heavy yet certain fingers
These children his but for a generation;
their father gone to service;
mother sells her wares
Such eager faces
Smiles bloom;
his patience boundless
He peels; one for her and one for him,
grateful, and with a love never fallow

What the Wind Hears

Scraping across branches,
whispering across grass,
sucking our voices from the sky.

Drowning sounds, stealing our words;
carry, scatter, and cry.

What does the wind imagine of our
conversations, our arguments,
our desperate shouts?

What sense of the single-sided phone call,
or does the wind hear both?

When the wind stops, do the words
drop from the sky like hail, or fall
like leaves, waiting for another breeze?

Stand Still

The morning's quiet is a perfect place.
A goddess must have arranged it so.
A quiet call of birds;
the weight of silence endures the sky.

It is ill to break such stillness;
words such a sin.
Best to accept these blessings
in full void of cacophony.

A cough destroys
the sound of sunlight landing
within the fog of breath.

It falls upon you
as dew freezing on leafy blades;
under the blossoming fullness
of an empty sky, it quiets the soul.
Stand still.

Quiet Days

Two months ago I lamented the lack of silence
between cars passing.

Never a full moment, never a breath
where the sound of one approaching,
or one leaving, did not intrude
upon the silence of wind in my trees,
or the quiet birds chattering in my yard.

Now I breathe long, stretching moments
where no car, motorbike, or truck
blemishes the peace.

Long moments I cherish
until the blare of the next ambulance.

Laughter in the Sky

Laughter in the sky

                    reaching

Leaves in the air

                    falling

Prints in the snow

                    going

Stones in the wall

                    resting

Hands in the folds

                    grasping

Laughter in the Sky

Tears in the sand

        touching

Laughter in the sky

        wondering

An Important Sky

Where do they fly,
lifted on silhouette wings; where do they fly,
those unfinished years?

Whose sound do they carry?
Has anyone marked the trails
of words lifting through clouds?
Has anyone found where the wind starts?

An important sky crushes
against my insignificant, unfinished years;
hounding my memories to
fall where the wind ends.

I stand under tomorrow's promise,
on ground built of granite
and rivers of April ice and
October's burned colors; I hope.

We burn through our days

An Important Sky

casting coals into our fires,
noticing not what fuel remains;
raging over our scorched loss.

And when they fly,
those unfinished years,
they leave nothing but unwashed light.

Bibliography

Thaw, originally published February 15, 2020 at AllPoetry.

A River Runs, originally published March 26, 2020 at Free Verse
Revolution.

Peeling Grapes, originally published April 16, 2020 at Free Verse
Revolution.

Quiet Days, originally published April 25, 2020 at HelloPoetry

Acknowledgments

My desire to write poetry came from reading other poets, such as Ursula K. Le Guin, Tarfia Faizullah, Allen Ginsberg, and Donald Hall. I have no idea what I take from these great poets, but I admire their work and attitudes. I was fortunate enough to hear Ginsberg read from his work, including *Howl*, and the experience lit a slow burning ember for poetry.

I also count as craft influence, *The Ode Less Travelled: unlocking the poet within*, by Stephen Fry, *How a Poem Moves*, by Adam Sol, and *Why Poetry*, by Matthew Zapruder.

In addition to the endless support of friends and family, I need to express my gratitude to those who read and encouraged my work at AllPoetry and HelloPoetry. To my readers on Instagram and my blog, thank you. Your support keeps me going.

Thanks to Kristiana Reed for publishing my work to a larger audience at Free Verse Revolution. And finally, thank you to Karen D. for reading the early draft of the collection. Trusted feedback is coffee for the writer's soul.

About the Author

Kevin J. Fellows was raised in the wilderness of New Hampshire's small towns and scattered forests. He lived in upstate New York for a spell and now lives with part of his family in the desert southwest. He played bass in a band during the 80s. In high school he wrote a speech entitled *The Meaning of Life*, his first and only foray into stream-of-consciousness verse.

If you enjoyed *An Important Sky* his short collection *Stitches* is available free. Or consider supporting Kevin's Patreon and receive poems and stories every month. He is the author of the forthcoming novel *At the End of the World*

For news and updates on all of Kevin J. Fellows' poetry and novels, sign up for the Infectious Magic Digest. Digest subscribers also receive cover reveals, occasional free poems and stories, and more.

Also by Kevin J. Fellows

Coming in 2020. *At the End of the World:* a novel by Kevin J. Fellows.

A wayward city spinning through time and place connects and draws travelers; trapping them with no way to return home. Each traveller, Nico the peddler, Stina the university graduate, João, Lieutenant for the King of Portugal, and Croydon, a boy at the edge of adolescence, must choose: stay in the strange medieval city where magic infects and wealth is not measured in coin, or leave to find a new home in the next time and place.

Many arrivals accept the city's magic, others desire all of it for themselves, and one seeks to destroy it. Disrupting the magic of the oasis could trigger the unmaking of the city and the world containing it.

Nothing but silence, heat, and wind. The road was empty except for João and King Sebastião. It could only be purgatory. "Perhaps," João said. "We really have died, and this is the realm of sleeping kings."

A rich, magical debut: a tale of finding ourselves in unfamiliar places and situations. The choices we face: do we find solace in what familiarity remains, or risk everything hoping to regain what we lost, or simply embrace the strange and the unknown?

To order, visit modernfolklorepress.com.

www.ingramcontent.com/pod-product-compliance
Lightning Source LLC
Chambersburg PA
CBHW021132080526
44587CB00012B/1246